LUCKY WITNESS

Poems by
Kathleen Lynch

BLUE LIGHT PRESS ◆ 1ST WORLD PUBLISHING

1ST WORLD
PUBLISHING

SAN FRANCISCO ◆ FAIRFIELD ◆ DELHI

Lucky Witness

1st World Library
PO Box 2211
Fairfield, IA 52556
www.1stworldpublishing.com

Blue Light Press
www.bluelightpress.com
bluelightpress@aol.com

Book & Cover Design
Melanie Gendron
melaniegendron999@gmail.com

Cover Photo
Onward, K. Lynch

Author Photo
E. Pandolfino

First Edition

Library of Congress Control Number: 2019937867

ISBN 9781421836263

For Eddie

LUCKY WITNESS — Table of Contents

PART I

Ophelia in Utah 9
Linoleum 10
The Hard Season 12
Only One Photograph 14
The Dream Speaks 15
Whistle 16
Cutting 17
Dream Threads 19
After Visiting the Cemetery 20
Tooraloora Lies 21
Selling the Tiger 22
Burglars 24
Arrangement of Boxes 25
Jacket in the Back of the Closet 26
Sacrifices 27
Nightwatch 28
Incubus 29
History Lesson 30
Outside Voices 31
Black Butterflies 33
Fully Alive 34

PART II

Seeing Something 39
Without Birds 40
Serious Weather 41
Castanets 42
Front Lawn 43
Canned Food Drive 45
Predawn Petition 47
Halloween 48

Sometimes I Feel I Understand 50
Farmer's Wife Turns Husband into Scarecrow 51
Today Please, No Poetry 52
Afterstory 54
Learning the Basics 55
Variegated 56
Letter to an Unmet Grandmother 58
Ineffable 59
A Question Occurs 61
You May Ask 62
Late at Night my Sister Told Me Stories 64
Sorry in Two Voices 66

PART III

Abracadabra 69
Old Math 71
Impossible 72
The Naturalists 73
Domestic Situation 74
Prowler 75
Word by Word 76
Hungry 77
Non-Cinematic Departure 78
It Was Dark When I Went In 79
Parting 81
Robe 82
Throes 83
Wind Shifts — A Letter of Sorts 84
Post-prandial Mood, Candles to the Nub 86
For the Morning and the Pain 87
Remission 89
True Geometry 90
Why I Love Oysters 92

About the Author 93

I.

OPHELIA IN UTAH

I lay down singing, down
in the glassy stream, my arms
laden with crow-flowers, nettles,
my mouth still telling prayer
and songs of grief, my mind,
they say, gone. O father,
brother, lover, those heavy
skirts and what I carried
bore me down, and under
green water I left you,
left you my body to plant.
Imagine my surprise
when not just time passed
but all space and dimension,
and I surfaced farther away
than you or I could ever imagine.
This is a lake of salt, where all tears
come to rest, and I am buoyant here,
bare under a very bare sky, completely
awake now, and curious. I carry nothing
but words. What have they named
the flowers in this windblown place?
Who will I meet if I rise up, walk
to the far road? I will say Here I am.
I will wear the one face God gave me.
The water is a vast breathing thing —
it grows dark beneath me. Dark
and deeper still.

LINOLEUM

She notices how closely the darkest shade
of the pattern matches her school shoes,
a color Mother calls oxblood.

She has been making pictures all morning
for her father to pack in his duffel bag
parked by the door. Already she has drawn

their house with its two front windows
like surprised eyes, the door
between them like an open mouth.

She drew Father and Mother standing on the lawn,
their stick arms reaching for the small stick arms
of three girls. She gave herself, the girl in the middle,

a yellow triangle of a dress. The sisters, blue.
She gave the yard a row of red tulips, where really
there was only dirt, but she had become good at tulips.

But now she is hunched in the kitchen, trying to draw
the way the old apricot tree looks through the window
where Father has toast and coffee. That's where he sat

a few weeks before, when the radio man, Gabriel Heater,
told important news in a voice that scared her.
The window she drew seemed crooked, seemed wrong,

and it was hard to fit such a large tree into it. While she
erased to make it better, a mockingbird began calling
from a nearby tree. It sang on and on, as if

it was telling in bird talk answers to a hundred
questions, repeating them patiently. She wished
she knew bird talk. She had so many questions.

If she could, she would ask it, How far away
is Korea? and, do they have to kill the ox
in order to get that color onto my shoes?

THE HARD SEASON

Rain-glutted, the stream
splays to the base
of the retaining wall.

Good. Now you have reason
to pray. Of all the birds
watching from winter-stripped

trees, vultures
are kindest, killing
nothing. This is a true

measure of things.
Don't hold back now, have
chocolate, throw extra

kindling on, even though
skies urge cover & hoarding.
When mice pitter in

for crumbs, compliment
their small feet and fitting
ways. When your mouth

houses a curse, swallow,
think how you once
had no words at all

yet managed
your hungers. Everything
that comes, passes.

Everything that passes
rakes its fingers through
and passes.

ONLY ONE PHOTOGRAPH

When you walked down the cellar stairs
you were not a grandmother and I was not
anything. When you reached for the bottle
from the ledge, I doubt you thought
of the possibility of me, or how your gesture
would seal your son — my father still a boy —
forever in that reaching.

There is one photograph. One. You wove
your red hair into a braid that day, coiled it
like a crown. I wonder what you felt then,
that let you take such care to loosen
two tendrils to curl at your temples
and let them fall, their tips pointing
down to the edges of your slight
smile. They say I have your mouth,
your high forehead. Now I have what
you could have had — your face
finding its way into greater age.
I carry your rarely told story —
and a full weight of questions
with their unknowable answers.

THE DREAM SPEAKS

1

Last night I came to you in perfection wearing the yellow dress you wore with your first heels, and the face you are achieving in the gathering of your years. That naked. You turned me into a worried remark in the morning, a *strangest thing*.

2

You walked across the field to Sunday Mass tilting in your spiked shoes, well aware of the neighbor mowing who paused and wiped his brow seeing you this way the first time. Small daisies stitched on your breast. Yellow, the wide bending grasses. Sky, blue.

3

You can go on not knowing me your whole short life. But I have moved every move with you. Crossing the field was not the beginning. Do you think I am nothing or so mere you can just throw a crust, a line here and there, a sigh?

4

You should say, *There was a woman in a dress I once wore, she looked dangerous, old, I got her by the wrists and twisted her into my armlock and saw she had two poisonous tips growing from the palm of her right hand and she smacked my face hard with it and I woke up.* Say: *I want you to meet her.*

WHISTLE

I may be indispensable. I may
be made of error. In either case
whatever I am will evaporate

like the whistle outside meant
to summon a dog. Perhaps
it came to its seeker.

Perhaps it entered the holy
zone of shadow, like the beloved
mutts of my childhood

who "disappeared." I did not
recognize the ritual.
I believed in the magic

of appearance
and its opposite. The realm
was not a stronghold.

I was willing to give myself
to dream or to the mirror.
I wore a clean white slip.

She said I should always be ready.

CUTTING

Bent serious with scissors, the girl
cuts from the wardrobe book a dream
life for her cardboard doll. The excess
of outfits compensates for tenuous fit

and the failure of tabs that weaken
from first fold.

Mother turns Bing over,

and on either side he sounds
happier than the radio man's
urgent bursts from Father's
portable piping in
from the fire escape.

Page after page fills with hollowed
shapes. Quietly the child amasses

a pocket-sized reality
of dreamed-for ruffles, taffetas,
rick-racked pinafores,
rompers edged with eyelet.

This is the kingdom she works
for the six inch smiling girl
whose chest and hips are laminated
on one plane; whose whole
self is blank on back.

Rompers. Even she knows
they belong to an erased

world. But she can see herself
in them, cartwheeling on some impossibly
wide lawn, all the guests clapping,

her parents proud, and hand in hand.

DREAM THREADS

My mother was a pinprick.
A tinny sound through fog.
Father, a hammer,
and indispensable. Or

was it the other way around?

The two of them were
the one of them. Like the rainbow
on the body of the trout
and the dark that shows it.

Before, each could lay claim
to some treachery. And each,
some enduring warmth.

Once they stood in fine air
with the intentions of lovers.

How is it so many things fall
out of kilter, stumble
like drunks at a wedding?

I dream them this mercy:
another place to breathe.

They come the great distance
death imposes without luggage,
articulate, apologizing for nothing.

They wear amazing clothes.

AFTER VISITING THE CEMETERY

I prefer this room, away from blistering
wind, away from strangers' eyes.
And I like that the table is round,
bare, sullied by my presence
alone. If tears come they come
like secrets, like the little disc
of the host melting on my tongue.
I thought it was God. I thought
it would feed me but never
felt full. I blamed my mother
for being a small human,
for turning cold in the heat
of that difficult house.
Today, in the white
hour of winter
I laid hothouse flowers
on stiff grass. I felt
like a trespasser. Wind
struck me — a kindness,
really, urging me home.
The radiator ticks metallic, almost
a comfort, almost like someone
sits across from me,
clicking her nails on the table.

TOORALOORA LIES

After he died he became Dead Saint Dad — at last a man
she could invent — no longer "mortifying," no longer "shanty"
or "pigs-in-the-kitchen-Irish." All his early years of drunken rages,
of careening night rides with us in PJs, or the later years
of brutal binges & bashed Christmas trees blurred into stories
she made pretty enough to mist her eyes in the telling.
"He didn't get an easy start in life," she'd say, "If I'd left him
he'd have ended up in the gutter." Even as they wheeled
his body from the back bedroom through the weeping living room,
the fable of his life began. By unspoken agreement, none of us
would be "guttered,' no "ill of the dead" uttered about us. Later,
when she entered her great abeyance, her sainthood began,
her "crown in Heaven" crusted with hard-won jewels. We've hummed
their farewell songs so long now, we barely remember the words.

SELLING THE TIGER

A man came back from the mountains with a tiger.

> I thought it would be bigger and more beautiful,
> his wife sniffed.

Well it's an older tiger, he said. It's been around.

> Just what we need, she groused, a tiger with mileage on it.

But it's rare, hardly anyone else will have one, he pleaded.

> Everyone will see how bedraggled it is, she shrieked. It's
> uglier than the coat you gave me six years ago. And it's not
> big enough for us.

It's big enough for me, the man cried, putting his head in the
tiger's mouth. Look.

> You can hardly turn your head in there she gasped. How will
> we both fit? Take it back.

I can't take it back he cried, All Sales Final!

> Then you will be selling the tiger she yelled. It stinks and it
> is ugly.

These people are ridiculous, the tiger thought. They will never
appreciate me.

> He swished his tail and yawned. At the widest part of his
> yawn, he slipped out of his body and went to town to place
> a classified ad.

Now look, the wife wailed, that hideous tiger has left me. How could you bring home a beast that abandons me this way?

(After Russell Edson)

BURGLARS

Crows came down in a flurry like black hats
tossed at a rally, and settled in the bare, dead
cottonwood. Every acorn stored there for winter
by woodpeckers, they took. Well, so what.

It is a something that is nothing
to the woodpeckers. Could have been fire.
Could have been a wind bent blinding
white and nuclear.

Last week someone sliced a screen, slid open
my closet, touched my blouses. Someone rough
and hurried, who took my bright baubles,
left shoe smudges on the rug, whorls on the glass.

Don't get your feathers in a ruffle, I tell myself.
It's a good thing, to have something worthy
of taking. Even gewgaws. And I do have a secret
store of things not a soul would want.

I think: If you need to hate the takers, hate them
only a little. And in the same breath forget them.
They have bodies too — and their own
stores of things. Someday, something

like a wind will hoot down
in a clamor of taking from them.
Bit by valued bit, we all
will give every last thing over.

ARRANGEMENT OF BOXES

One, tipped over, empty.

~

One labeled Tongues of Martyrs, sealed.

~

Another filled with poems
found in dead soldiers' pockets.
It says: Assorted Poems - GIs.

~

Others closed, unmarked.

~

They are arranged in a room
walled with mirrors. Light
from above and below.
No shadows.

The Onlooker cannot detect
whether they are filled with medals
or ears or sacks of black
blood, congealing.
Or nothing.

Not without coming close.
Not without touching.
And opening.
And becoming reflected.

JACKET IN BACK OF THE CLOSET

In my first life, a man with rough hands
and soothing voice took me out to the world
that shines. He kept peppermints
in the right pocket for his boy.

Once the boy wept hard beside him,
while grayish mist fell on all gathered there.
The man pulled the child near, whispered,
"Prayer helps," and held him close.

The boy, now a man, has come for me today.
I will cover him as though
holding him. I long to be in the place
where the old man will rest,

to hear them sing and speak of grace.
But most of all, I ache to be of use,
to savor brisk, clean air, to stand
in clear light. To breathe.

SACRIFICES

The poem said: Now we must all eat beautiful women.

The poem-cutter cut out that line
and took it home. He read it over and over
then sautéed the words in butter

and ate them.

He ate them and now he is stuffed
with the words he has learned by heart.
He has learned a new hunger
that is an old hunger
and he is covered with shame.

The mother with the book of poems
found that the line was gone,
carefully sliced and taken away.
She knew it meant danger.

She knew it meant danger
so she locked her beautiful daughter
in the closet telling her:
There is a man out there in the moonlight
who is covered with shame.

She locked her daughter in the dark room
and every night now she lays a small poem
on the porch. *Eat this*, she says,
There are no beautiful women
in this house.

NIGHTWATCH

The hyenas of sleep
gather snapping
their necessary teeth.

My desolate bed
reminds them of the Serengeti
A smell in the air tells them

something is wounded.
Their jaws open
with the low whoops

of natural excitement.
They all freeze
at the sight of my pale body

falling through the startling night
falling to the dry white grass, opening
arms and legs to their

unembarrassed stares.
The sounds settle. The dogs
begin to move.

INCUBUS

And it came to my bed
and lay upon me. It pressed
on my body and stretched me
full length. It wrapped me
three times round and turned me
every way of turning.
It spit hot exotic spumes
of breath all about my face
and its voice came from a place
deep in my brain: *Wake*, it spat,
Wake to this. And it turned me
over and shoved its thumbs
beneath my blades, wrenched
at them, oh, the pain,
and someone yelled, *Wings!*
And it took all I had
to fling it off, to turn my body
back to the pose of sleep.
And I never said a word.
Never opened my eyes.

HISTORY LESSON

"Foy-Yay" is how Mother Michelle pronounced
it. Her rule: no groups of more than three girls
could gather, gossip, chat within that space.

Our oldest nun, Mother Felician, said
"Go on, girls, talk among yourselves. I'll watch
and warn when she draws near the foyer doors."
We whispered, complicit, spread news
from group to group like actors' hissed asides.

And yet we made such mock of that old nun — so
rumpled, so unkempt. Her ragged flesh sagged
around her wimple like dying petals; her voice rasped
and quaked with age. Once she brought a seventy-eight
to play for History class — a Mozart mass
introducing the chapter when he lived.

Mother Felician went into a kind of trance, paced
desk aisles, hummed, then sang some Latin words,
eyes shut, jowls atremble. Tears streamed
her creases. Something shifted inside me
and I prayed she couldn't hear giggles and
shuffled chairs while students twisted to share
the muffled hilarity of that scene.

I didn't understand why I myself
wept walking home alone remembering
how her waxy hand marked the air as if
lifting notes straight out of the phonograph
offering them to each of us as gifts.
It's as alive to me now as it was then.

OUTSIDE VOICES

At the still point, the moment
turned vivid: the priest's white square

at his throat left a mild abrasion.
His shoes shone in the dark way

wet stones shine. His waxy hands
inspected each other. *Send her away,*

he said. *I'll give you a reference.*

Outside, the voices of children sounded

like the outside voices of children —
muffled, unreal. Now there would be

one less of them. My old life, which
had seemed, until that moment, new,

was taken by one great inhalation
into the lungs of the priest — a smoke

made of me. I did not speak. I deserved.
They murmured about cover stories,

tickets, arrangements on the other end.
On the other side of the window, a young

house finch nicked at the ledge. The rectory
cat stretched and arched in a shrinking patch

of sun. Down below, in the chapel, I knew
women were crossing themselves, plinking

dimes into the candle bank, all of them
down on their knees praying.

BLACK BUTTERFLIES

Why do you keep talking
on the phone? We cut
this vision before you, swoop
over your lawn, a frenzied cloud,
a million wings at your window,
then go on our way.
You sit there talking
instead of stepping out among us.
You say *Something is happening*
with the butterflies. You must be rich
and completely sure of yourself.
You must know how many days
are left, how many chances remain.

FULLY ALIVE

for Quinton

Today I loved everybody. Not in the generic
I'm-a-nice-person way, but actually. Acutely.
I loved the baby-faced dentist as he lowered
the air-drill burr into my mouth to grind
away uneven tips of my molars.

The grating whirr made enamel dust puffs float
like winter breath, rise, evaporate. More of me
disappearing, I thought… then feared, what if
the soul is in the teeth, but my mind, which always
chats me up, even on idle, countered, No…
more people lose their teeth than their souls.

This is the most fully alive I've felt since you left.

When leaving the parking lot, I loved the semi-
Asian, semi-blind old man who tapped his way
to the alley's edge and waited as I exited. I hadn't
seen him behind the shrub, but he stood, safe,
all his remaining senses attuned. I loved the ragbag
woman at the corner, filthy, wrecked, talking
loudly to no one, though maybe she saw
a compassionate listener I could not detect.

I love the birches outside my window. In a way,
I think of them as people, bending to every weather.
Lately, when they are smitten with glisters of rain,
I speak your name aloud in my silent room.

Most of all, I love the mirage people, those who
closely resemble you. When I see them, I think… Oh!
Then… Oh. They crop up everywhere now —

bus stops, restaurants, grocery aisles. This is the new
mystery of you — being "gone" yet achingly present.
I count that among your many gifts to us: poems,
love, great laughter — things that abide. Like the sound
of your name — that particular, cherished song.

II.

SEEING SOMETHING

Our mother undressed
beneath her nightgown,

arms pulled in to save us
from seeing something.

I never saw her naked.
Blessed be

those parts of her body, the
secrets worth keeping.

Mystery of breasts.
The slow, substantial sway of them

beneath a housedress.
The give.

I filled nickel rainbow pads
with pretty ladies in hourglass

gowns. Sometimes I made myself
fall to draw a scrape of blood. I cried

hard enough to be held
a little while against her chest:

Yardley's Lavender & the sweetest
forbidden. I kept my eyes shut.

I don't know what kind of look
she wore on her face.

WITHOUT BIRDS

Any insomniac can tell you
that without birds
the world would stay dark forever —
that blackness is lifted
first by their round coos and churtles,
then creaks & chirps
& rising racket. What effort
to change the earth this way!
To do it always, and on time!
The heaviness of houses
means nothing to them.
They sing back color. Black bushes bloom
their various greens. Gold gone black
turns gold again. And the weary human
at the window shapes up distinct,
a survivor, lucky witness
to the calling up of light.

SERIOUS WEATHER

This time you say Look how wet
the world is. Roofs are stepping stones
in brown ponds. Hang paintings
higher in the museum. Keep
your galoshes by the door. Or don't

say anything. Water goes
on flowing. On every channel
they count how many days now
tell about their lives
just sunk. Just washed away.
Everything. Everything. The same

as when the sky spreads its broad
blue sponge & takes it all back.
Whole families
of corn stalks crackle
dry pathetic tunes in blanched
fields. Lips of the lakes
pull back and back and back. Front
page states how long we've gone on
like this. You say: Look how dry
the world is. You say
Oh when will this ever end?

CASTANETS

for Gloria

Leafless birches sag with winter catkins
which allows more room for a blue
December dome to scoop
the scenery. This is not theater but
yet another page torn from
the calendar. Our albums
are filling with dead people
whose smiles remain as bright
as their holiday sweaters.

We were twelve and she was already full-
breasted. I still wore braids and prayed
daily for something more than a "chest."
I can see us now — young, silly, laughing
with our Pepsis & sunflower seeds,
rooting from bleachers for boys in Pony
League. They called me Olive Oyl,
but said she was "stacked," "built"
and tried to get her to touch
her elbows behind her back.

When our team entered the field we
bolted up cheering as the cutest boy,
the one we both loved, took the mound
and wound up for the pitch. As we settled,
I leaned to Glo, said,

"When I'm all grown, I'll dress like
a Spanish Dancer, I'll swirl and flash,
wear the reddest lipstick and these boys
will want me like nobody's business."
She spat a few shells, hooted a joyous
laugh, grabbed my wrist and said
"I'll buy you castanets!"

FRONT LAWN

Someday I will have a life
without these edges, these
pathetic brown patches.

I will open the door on a meadow,
a wild spread of anything that wants to grow
anywhere it wants to. Nothing

will be shorn. I will sow nothing.
I will not import water.
I will open the door

and walk right out.
Let the neighbors talk.
I will stand there

innocent as Van Gogh
in his fields.
And as terrified.

This will mean everything
has changed. This will mean,
after I count the birds

and brush the whiskered necks
of poppies, after I press
spikes of thistle

into my thumb-tips,
that it is time for me
to lie down.

This will mean that I am there
and there is nowhere
left to go.

CANNED FOOD DRIVE

We lived in the lucky world —
not the far place where flies

sipped at eye corners
of children too weak to cry.

A camera showed that world to us
on posters. But we were children.

We wanted most to not be those
others, with their terrible bones.

We spoke of them wide-eyed, with
what we thought was tenderness.

But our words came in a different register,
as if to speak of such betrayal

by the grown world could bring
a harm of great immensity

upon us too. We got to choose
from the cupboard. We gave

what we hated — beets, peas,
mushrooms. Our dreams

were not of rice. The moon
laid light on our bicycles propped

against the porch. Sycamores
became our giants standing guard;

the overgrown shrub, our fort. We thought
we understood what was required.

Even crouched beneath our desks
during drill, we said one prayer

for the fear, one for recess.
McClellan Air Force Base

sent forth big-bellied planes
that rattled the windows

of our houses. Evenings, we took
to the streets, shrieking

with joy, rode madly fast
around the block. We collapsed

on the lawn breathless, the earth
cool beneath us & pounding hard

as if it had one great heart.
As if it was ours.

PRE-DAWN PETITION

May fog hold its breath close on me.
May the cur-dogs of my most sorrowful
dreams curl together in one safe nest.
Let chill remind me I am flesh.
Let me always know flesh is the gift
of my broken faith.
Let body keep faith with what
body needs, and all bloods
and wires flow and charge and cross
safely. Let the excellent deeps
of my ears hark, hark! to the rising
thrumming day, both blessed
and cursed. Let this paltry prayer
for myself become vapor, take
to air and enter the mist of our city's
morning, anoint the lids of all
who are stricken, all
still sleep-struck.

HALLOWEEN

means a mouth
cut to shape a smile.

Relieved we are
that the dead fly up

and away — and
horrified when they

don't. It's elemental.
We need a face

to express the hidden
face. Mother opens

her mouth around
the imagined spoon

while she feeds
mush into the learning

infant mouth. We,
who have fed

the dead into holes, once
painted and garbed ourselves:

look what monsters
we are, what fabled

beauties, what fierce
Ninjas. Can you spare

a little something?
A sweet thing?

For me? For
a child?

The whole night
made of doors.

SOMETIMES I FEEL I UNDERSTAND

nothing, not even the five yellow leaves
I carried home while walking the dog, each
larger than my hand, nearly the size of
my face, and unknown to me but as "leaf."

And the dog the whole way strained,
intent and eager for new information —
some scent conveying character
or danger. Once, she eagerly approached
a drying scat, then backed up stiffly,
neck hairs spiked.

How many messages besiege us
just outside our range? What alarms
do we fail to detect? I was born
to be harmed, I know that. Born to be
eaten and killed, killed and eaten,
like all the others. This is our bond. As we
broke from the blood of a body, we will
break again. Between the great breakings

there is song after song, hurt
and work, failings that leave their
scent too, and the dumb unclaimed
things, like walking the dog late
in late October, carrying home
five large leaves fallen from a tree
whose name I have yet to learn.

"FARMER'S WIFE TURNS HUSBAND INTO SCARECROW"

– Tabloid headline –

Really, it was the near weightlessness.
And really, that I wanted him
outside but not too far away.

Doesn't he look a bit like Christ —
arms straight out like that and nothing
but air all around?

You think you know someone
and then they surprise you.
Even after thirty-two years.

Thought I'd never get his huge chair
into the garage. It had to go —
so sagged and sprung and stained.

Summer's done. Petals are littered
all around him. Practically nothing left
worth protecting.

Look at him flap and flutter,
going nowhere. I should tell the crows
he's harmless now. Just rags. Sticks. Straw.

TODAY, PLEASE, NO POETRY

no nuance, shadow
or light. I'm so tired

of everything meaning
something. Let me leave

the curtains drawn,
stay in my robe

all day and watch
All My Children

The Edge of Night
One Life to Live.

Let the music say
This Bud's For You

You Deserve a Break
Today. I do, you know.

I'm cursed just looking
at the laden bookshelf

noticing Sanctuary
leans against

As I Lay Dying.
I want to lie all day

on this couch
without remembering

that my children
are grown & gone

their beautiful faces
moving in rooms

hundreds of miles
from here;

that last week
my beloved

Sojourner
died here in my arms

and I laid her on moss
deep in Santa Cruz

woods. Nature is terrible
and I don't like weather

that reminds me of anything
but it always does.

I'm doomed, you see
to get up and go down

each day trying
to make something of it.

AFTERSTORY

They've been coming, lately,
through the long haul the dead
traipse to reach the unmoored
boat of my dreams. Furled in sleep,
I can only puzzle at their youthful
shapes as they jabber away, nonchalant,
familiar with me, but not all that
interested. She was my mother, but
clearly before that something else, and after,
well, so much of her own making.
Her husband, my father, for all the stories
he told his rapt children, all his rages
& dramatic sweeps, seems finally plain,
more compliant, almost pleased to be
offstage. His voice croons, sweeter
and subdued. And she, once labeled
"lace curtain," prim, has allowed a wild glint
show in her eyes, and loosed
her long-again hair to the designs
of strange and changing weather.

LEARNING THE BASICS

In the midst of it all —
good laughs, work
children, funerals
friends, and lovers who
finally do leave,
we must count ourselves

lucky to have been born
with what we need: mouth,
anus and the blind heart
slugging away steadily
in its cage.

The exchange is simple:
food for life — our life
held in the small fist &
released, the rhythm
basic, sufficient.

Burning black and shiny
the Heart gloms its own
light, taken from bone
from luminous blood
& the molten center.

Daily it descends
to night & trundles
through dreams back
to the surface. This
is the slow pulse
of a whole life lived
in one body.

VARIEGATED

I used to fear nothing was large enough to hold me. Now nothing
small enough. Though sound can be a container

of sorts. For instance, one short passage in the mockingbird's
exhaustive litany. I waited for it to come around again and it did.

Damsel flies couple in frenzied clouds above the pond. Shimmer
as if a bride ripped off her veil and flung it there.

Blackberries surge at the edge, dense, and, some say, an invasion.
Willows drape and flutter, hold off blunt sun

in all but the smallest winking holes. The watery sound of tires
on asphalt flows through. It too is a music I've grown used to.

Once we had no names for the things that turned us this way,
then that. Lulled. Or sparked panic,

which I now can call *killdeer in the bulldozed lot*. Staccato.
Sharp, skittering and fierce. Hopelessly.

To be here again as one who knew no names. Who reached
into the tangle regardless of thorns. Thin blooms of blood on the arm

tasted like one good thing. The juice the other. Stains on hands
and mouth deep and good too. Marked us as ragged saints.

Seen from high above, our heads might have looked like variegated
blossoms, bobbing. Together and sometimes alone.

What if the word landscape means danger? Appropriation
in the minds of the Takers. Yet, look how peaceful the golf course:

our made thing. Curved and clean. Smooth. Soothing.
Surface a green infant. And, yes, I admit: pretty.

LETTER TO AN UNMET GRANDMOTHER

They said there was nothing of yours left
but I found a black and white under the lining
of a rat-gnawed jewelry box. Until now you existed
only in stories, the hardest one the slow-leaked
secret about your suicide. First, I thought you look
too strong for someone who would do that, but
I know deep things are never that simple, and guess
it's more about luck, or something nameless.

Now I'm a grandmother myself — *Maga* to our flourishing
boys. I've seen seven decades of family history unreel
with its tangles and splices. But as a child I believed
that if only I'd known you, if you'd waited for me
to come along, I'd have been able to charm or cheer you
out of it. I'd pretend we'd come to visit, and you'd rush us
with your wide embrace, and somehow I'd be the one
who would end up on your lap, and you'd untwine my
waist-long braids, brush and brush until my hair
rose up electric to meet your hand.

That dream's behind me now, but the afterlife of its wish
burrowed in as if it had come true. I will say this: I love
knowing that once you carried my mother in your body,
and she was born with half of me in her, and that means
in a way I lived in you once, like a picture waiting in an
undeveloped roll. And the dog in the photo — your dog
I suppose. How gently you lean to the mutt, offer a treat
from your apron. I can almost see you stroke her ruff
in the next frame; almost hear you coo, *Good girl, good girl.*

INEFFABLE

I've gone ancient on myself,
timeless in time, back to the garden
of rocks, to a rough place where nearly
no thing of worth takes purchase.
They stood there too, I know — the old ones,
the gone. Torrent of time slipping — out,
away, lost, leaving the body
dumb and hollow as a cave.

I'm done looking for solace
in the rise and fall of day or night,
done listening to the mythic
wishes of my duplicitous mind
I hauled myself weary, out-of-shape,
climbed scabrous cliffs, crawled dark
beaches, clambered through caverns
and into rain slashing, into black
blackening, and over bodies — all
those bodies no longer in need
of their names. I spit this passage
of metaphor out of my mouth.

I close my eyes against the sky's
evidence, and don't know if it shines
glassy pink or brutal red, or soothing red,
or stupid pink, or any other inconclusion.

Ineffable, to be wrenched from air in capacious
lungs, from touch with its continuous electric
stabs of brilliance and hum of comfort,
from sight & its million fractals of light,
from mind with its dreams, its complications.

I don't know enough of anything yet,
cannot even name which bird intrudes
right now with its sparkling declaration.

Even if there is no sound where the gone ones
have gone, no way to know song from stone,
I raise my flat voice to the vaulted sky
and for them I sing most horribly, most loud,
most surely in vain, of my approach.

A QUESTION OCCURS:

Will I ever reel again?
Loose and mad
with love, and willing
to lose everything?
I remember the light
of it, and a distinct hum.

The room wobbled
around the water-bed.
The stray puppy slept
at the foot, at sea. And I,
a brute, floated
in that madness — that
gangster getaway
we fell into. Today,

decades later, I think
of that rampage of touch
perfected. The tremor
and tenor of our voices.
Cries. What bright
beasts we were,
cultivating a joy
worthy of grief.

YOU MAY ASK

Who will tell you the meaning of the rain
      when it comes down in slabs, when
      it appears in the middle of a sun-sodden
      day unpredicted and atypical, when
      it bashes the longing meadow grasses
      into whorls that look like a body
      fell and thrashed before disappearing
      and the rain matches exactly the heavy
      liquid horror you have been hauling
      in the brimful bowl you are afraid
      to set down, afraid to drink
      every breath a measured threat and who
      will tell you if you will ever sleep again

Who keeps opening the door no matter
      the weather and tries to lead you
      through corridors and alleys
      great vibrating halls of trees
      as you stumble resisting, crying
      no I won't look, don't make me
      but there it is anyway at your feet
      broken-winged and stricken
      you knew all along it was out there, knew
      it was hurt, it belonged to you, and who
      will steady your hand when the only way
      to tell if the hurt thing still has breath and pulse
      is to touch it

Who will wait beside you when you stand
      stunned cold and glad you have done
      what was asked, not in a brave golden
      way but reluctant and cringed low like

a small thing, yes, you may be one who
trembles and weeps while the moon
snakes over trees, while trees bend
helping the night moan as you
turn and turn all four ways wondering who
will peel your wet things off and lift you
carry you now

LATE AT NIGHT MY SISTER TOLD ME STORIES

For Pat

She drummed the wall unspooling
stories in the shadow-thick room
where a stitch of light from beneath
the door showed us enough of nothing.

Whole horses loomed in corners.
The possibility of wolves. I remember
the breath and smell of it. The bloom
of her voice against voices

raised in the other room. Breathing
and creaks rose from the other bunk —
the little ones finally slept. My heart
banged as if it might propel me

away on the raft of my body
out of fear-logged shallows,
the stifle of my imaginings.
Kings entered the room. Heroes

who were kind to children swung
like zoo monkeys from bed
to bed. Women laughed loudly
in bars, and stood up to sheriffs.

They had no husbands.
They had unimaginable lives.
One thing ran into another,
her voice and the pictures

slowed, the room became ancient,
a cave of breath. I gave myself over
to the whole of it: rhythm
and thrum, my sister's stories,

those changeable outcomes.

SORRY IN TWO VOICES

1

Turkey with burst breast
skin. The warped door's
drag over the rug. He's gone
for pies, everyone else
hunched at the TV. This
is my chance alone
with you, little holiday
mother, in the scuff
and chaos childhood
kitchen, to ask the question
that has rung the blood meat
out of my bones, has hummed
my head dry and swollen
for a decade: are you sorry
you put me in that cab,
in that room with cracks
and stink and silence?
That you didn't fling open
your arms like wings and wrap
me, seal my lank, gravid
girl frame back to your body?
Are you just going to stand
there, stiff back to me, and stir
and stir as if my words
were nothing, even now?

2

Again the breast too dry. Who
knows how long before he's back
with his sacked bottle and surl,
and how many more years
must I lift a big dead thing
from the oven with the rotted
seal, sprung thermometer?
Air in this room makes me
dizzy, or is it some sagged
brain tube finally giving
way, and wouldn't that be
something: to go flat out in
the middle of the Big Feed,
all of them grown, but even
so, still huddled and groaning
for me to fill the trough
again. Oh I was once young
with hands so fine a catalog
showed them holding dainty things.
Veins, now. Wrinkles. Claws.
I'm dizzy and one grown girl
is at my ear with breath
catching over some old lack
in me. At least the gravy
thickens to a good dark gloss.

III.

ABRACADABRA

When our mother yelled *Stop that or I'll box*
your ears! I thought she meant chop them off
and put them in a Roi Tan cigar box.

A few years later, a local State Fair side-
show magician sawed a pretty older girl right
through the middle. We screamed, yet she

danced back to us, all smiles and sequins, her
breasts bouncing the way I hoped mine would
someday — a transformation I prayed for daily.

When mom wrung her hands over her many
& various worries, hissing *I'm simply beside myself,*
I tried to picture that diaphanous other version

of our mother — not a ghost, but not all there like
a real body — a magic vapor-mother who mimicked
her hand-wringing, pacing and contorted face,

always beside her. Years later, when I knew something
more about metaphor, she told me *You've lost your head*
when I married him and brought him home.

Fast forward to a woman, me, in our bed decades
later, now master of my own arts of appearance
and disappearance, and my cold acquaintance

with how close one can come to death and not die.
He sleeps, never sees my subterfuge when I grab my
head by its sturdy helmet skull, give it a good

crank to the right, lift it and set it on the nightstand.
Head is my night watchwoman, observant crone.
She stays alert, enjoys the way moonlight limns

our bodies — his, thirty years later, still lean, sinewy
bent to my shape; mine, slumped, rounded, in the pose
of a person asleep but, really, quite beside myself.

OLD MATH

Mr. and Mrs. found a squalling thing in their bed between them.
Put it in a bureau drawer, Mrs. said. What is it? asked Mr.
Call it One. It's One. A short year later Mrs. found another.
That's Two, he said. I'll put it in a crib with One.
It went on like that — Three came, then Four, all within six years.
One and Two and Three and Four were getting bigger. So was Mrs.
Mr. bought two metal bunk beds from the base, so One and Two
and Three and Four could sleep in the tiny other room.
When Five came, Five's crib was moved in with the bunks.
Not much later, Six came, and Five had a crib mate.
Then came Six and a Half, which went away in a bucket.
One, Two, Three, Four, Five, Six grew and changed, and seven
years later, everyone was surprised that Seven came, even
Mr. and Mrs. All of them loved Seven and Mrs. said Seven
came from Heaven. They all liked that idea, maybe because
the words rhymed. Then all of them got bigger and older
and finally Mr. and Mrs. went away as far away as going away
could take them. So One and Two and Three and Four and Five
and Six and Seven had only each other left. Among them they had
disappointments, jealousies, betrayals, sickness and sorrows, but also
uncountable joys. Laughter came in exponential torrents, when tears
came, the weepers found there really is strength in numbers. Add
One and Two and Three and Four and Five and Six and Seven
together, the total is twenty-eight. And, counting the others who
came to dwell with the original seven, that means twenty-eight
places to set at Thanksgiving tables, twenty-eight unwrapping gifts
beneath a tinseled tree. That's how it goes with numbers —
multiplication, division, and inevitable subtraction.
That's the way of things. The sum and summary of it.

IMPOSSIBLE

No question of the body
not knowing
its place in this, its way
of moving, plying.
Its way of opening.
Impossible to think
it had ever known
any other way
of being. Hands
with their great
restlessness, their
seeking. Legs,
their inner hollows.
Mouth and mouth.
Skin and its pressures,
its blooming flush.

THE NATURALISTS

Already lonely
for the beasts
we forgot to love
we try to learn
their habits, the secrets
they breathe into the last
cold morning. We notice
that even our own wet noses
push out small clouds
disappearing.

DOMESTIC SITUATION

The man who once wanted everything now wants
only his small room and a good radio.

His wife made yellow curtains edged with orange rickrack
for his windows. But now,
she wants the world.

The woman decides she is not a vessel, nor rib-sprung.
Oh, she feels. Oh.

Something furred and indifferent stirs in the shrubbery.
Oaks shrug their ancient shoulders while sun climbs
turning morning to noon to after.

The woman thinks: I have earned every line on my face.
I am due something.

She holds an apricot against her lips. The gold blush skin
feels like the flesh of a young lover. Her eyes close.

The juice tastes good going down. The pit —
a small, hard fact — lands in the garbage.

I won't excruciate any longer, she thinks.
I'll… I'll leave. Could I be one of those women
who… just… go?

Not far away, the sea continues its devotion
to departure and return.

He dials the ball game louder… something
exciting is about to happen.

PROWLER

The word itself moves
sideways through blood.
He works his way
along the darkened wall
to your window.
He finds the place
and waits
watches you
breathe in your sleep.
His breath comes from his
tight chest
slowly.
He is no voyeur.
A small sweat breaks out
in his gloved hands.
They are steady.
He is coming in.

WORD BY WORD

for Jim Garvey (1919 – 1999)

He holds his hands toward
fire. He has come in from rain

and is remembering rain.
He says torrent, runnel,

drench, quietly, to have
the words in his mouth.

In this way he loves
his life. Unction of oiled

ash. Yes. Treblinka
which sounds like a bell

but is not. He is willing
to carry it too. All the way.

Rain. Fire. Or the sun
of his wife's voice

offering an apricot.
Yesterday. Or twenty

years earlier. The gauze
of her blouse. Plume

of crimson in the fruit.
He takes them with his eyes,

his mouth. Holds and turns
each element carefully. Carries

the best to the desk.
Hands them back over.

HUNGRY

Is this why God made us human
and opposed our thumbs:
so we could climb
through centuries of knowledge and geometry
back to the place we knew first —
newborn, blind & only by instinct
nuzzling to suck
what would hold us here?

And isn't it this specific life we crave
as animals crave hot flesh brought down
to death in their mouths?
Not me — but some other simple beast
filling their jaws and falling.

I must admit I love
the hyenas' ravenous gorging,
the carrion birds above,
everything hovering
over delicious death.
But not mine.
Not yet.

NON-CINEMATIC DEPARTURE

Actually she leaves on a Greyhound.
Actually no one comes to stop her.
The children cry and pee.
One gets gum stuck in his hair.
His brother gets diarrhea
while they wait between buses.
Everyone hot and wretched.
The bus reeks of breath. Exit ramps
blur by. The boys kick seat backs
and each other. Finally they slump
tangled in exhaustion. She dozes.
In her dream somewhere near Fresno
things are different: She's in a dining car.
The children sleep sweetly in their berths.
Two daisies tremble in the vase by the window.
Tea is steeping in a fat white pot when he enters.
It is a wordless exchange. He sees everything
in her face. He understands why she must leave.
Never raises a hand. You can tell by his eyes
he forgives her. Wheels turn rhythmically.
She's rocked deeper asleep, then jostled
awake. Every scene the window offers
it takes away.

IT WAS DARK WHEN I WENT IN

and in the shaft dark. Hot. Dusty.
And dark when I came out again
and I was covered black and I hurt.
My hands, they did. And arms and back.
My eyes filled with grit and I wanted to lie down,
even in that crowded house. They chose me because
I am short and strong. Perfect for their mine tunnels.
I worked half-bent twelve hours each day for three pennies pay.

I stayed there longer than I thought I would
but was able to send money home,
paid for a grand slate for my mother's grave.
I came back to Galway a man and waited
for my brothers, gone to America. Australia.
I did not know where.
They never came back. Bless them
if they are still with us.

I got a wife, a hellcat of the first order,
older than me, barren.
The Troubles made her hard, I think.
But her scones took up honey better than any
and her pig stew could make a man
break out singing. She's long dead,
and bless her, wherever she be.

And I worked whatever work came my way, laid up
stones for kin-farm fences, cut and hauled silage,
dug dripping logs of peat from bogs
and stacked them to dry.
I liked to build the piles in a careful way,
liked looking back from the edge of the moor

at those mounds lined up like black cottages.
I tried not to be prideful, but they looked good to me
and I built hundreds of them. Hundreds.

Once I walked home from the drygoods store
with three other boys from town
and two Black and Tans stepped out from the trees
and they were drunk, madmen sure, and they shot
everyone but me. I remember
the crack of the guns and the laughter.
It is a good guess why the Lord spared me,
gave me so many days
and blessed me.

Now I am the oldest one in this village
and I have everything I need. I live
in a ward house on church property.
Women from the Altar Society bring me cakes and bread.
There is butter in my box and two kinds of jam.
I walk up the road for a draw of ale each night
and days I sit before the door, open so I can see
the sun come and go. The rain. So I can see
anyone who passes, anyone who turns up the path
to come see me. And bless them
whoever they be.

In memory of John Finnegan (1895-1992)

PARTING

It is best to watch people
leave when they go: follow
the shape of the old car turning
the last bend you can see. Stand there
hauling up sobs, your face in your hands.

So. Another part of your life unhooks
and drifts away. In the sharp sun your hands
look much older and so strange. You raise one
and wave into the quiet and settling dust.
You are the only one who sees this gesture;
the one who knows what it means.

ROBE

Stick to the right wall at all times.
Get ready for this pretty picture:
one of those cringing down mornings
slow and gelling and hesitant.
Pour in some color — cerise,
honey-monk gold, saffron —
everything locked in the sun's eye.
Roll and pitch and string it up.
Hold on for dear life, here comes
the father. In his big blue robe.
Under the weather. Don't be afraid,
little May Queen. You're not alone.
There's a dog in every room.
And one at the door
to guard the marriage.
Two in the yard to eat the dead.

THROES

The saint flung himself
into a thorn bush to incur
wounds worthy
of his joy.

Beyond what he imagined,
petals broke loose — so like
flesh he could not
look upon them.

Everything pushed
toward him: air, the ocean
hauling onto the edge, the shifting
medieval light.

Who knows sanctity of half-closed eyes?

Blessed be blood and its metallic
taste. Blessed the fool who flings
himself sick into the fever
of miracle.

Take his hands. Turn palms up: no
lines — not life, nor love, nor children.
This is not a silence, but a music
beyond the range.

If his wounds need binding,
rend your shirt
and bind.

WIND SHIFTS — A LETTER OF SORTS

after "The River-Merchant's Wife: A Letter"

You would not be happy with the way
the yard looks now — a shambles,
overgrown and flung every which way.
Wind lifted the umbrella right out of the table,
tossed it across the patio.

No one expected this turn
of weather. With all our instruments
we can still be surprised. If you were
still here, you'd be out there
wrestling — chasing branches, tying
new shafts of foxglove to stakes.

Radio reports a forest fire
out of control in Canada: *Wind
whipped, veering wildly, eating up
miles.* What is it like up there,
so far north? I can't picture you
in a place I've never seen. Is your
mailbox a slot in a door? What
do you see from your back window?

Funny how the deep things
between people just float away.

The umbrella rolls back and forth
on its stem over by the Bird of Paradise
which has grown huge, even though
I didn't amend the soil or feed it
the way you told me to. You should
see this — everything flapping
and flying around like some kind
of wild, un-peopled party.

Yesterday, two kinds of Orioles
at the feeder: Hooded and Bullock's.
Such a short time they can be seen together
in this zone. The Hooded doesn't range
any farther north. The other, well,
you've seen the breeding map:
red from Guatemala
all the way to Alberta.

POSTPRANDIAL MOOD, CANDLES TO THE NUB

Now I am practicing my day of pewter
when sky and water match
metal. Wind strips the oldest
book of its covers. According
to the story I will look like that —

like the bone basket of fish on the cleared
plate: Fence. Teeth. Needles.

Let me leave with seeds of light falling from me.
Let every song and curse I know
join the air-borne. Let each bullet
of my rare and fabulous rage
be poured silver, molten
into the waiting.

Yes, I am afraid. Yes
my tears are an amplitude.
When the light begins waving
its veils, let me breathe in that null
air, as if it could feed me,
could finally make me full.

FOR THE MORNING AND THE PAIN

Bone spur into the nexus. This too is the gift
I was saved for. Ripley's should include such

quiet human monuments of endurance, along with
those lifetimes of rubber bands amassed, or the hugest

ball of twine hulked in a garage, dwarfing a car.
I knew a man who devoted his life to the art

of entering pain. The wilderness in him asked for it.
It became a faith, to endure the insertion of needles.

Then nails. To breathe them through first pierce,
through flesh moved by metal, slowly opened —

his mind reeling its opposites — saying, No,
this is not how you felt as a child, this is only

metal and the perishable, penetrable membrane.
I want a talent like that: to become approximate

to the darling doomed body, but alien to it too.
In fairy tales, there would be some kind

of spell, some poke-pocus-shamana-hocus.
Blood pricks would become stolen rubies;

tears an ointment for the rite of standing
beside oneself. Let me cultivate the white-hot-

red-shot field of this inexorable landscape.
Let me welcome each morning, with its birds

and electrocutions, and thank it for arriving.
Let body, my favorite animal, listen

to my pleas, take this brick of salt I offer,
taste it, lie down beside me, and sleep.

REMISSION

All winter the young maple held on
to one red star of a leaf

and now its branches which reach as high
as her third story window sport hard

pale bud cases where crumpled
green stars sleep. They know nothing

of the unfolding into air, the reptile grasp
of finch and jay on limbs, or sun-tossed

baffles of wind from the bay.
Rapid Transit trains slide in and out

on tracks just below. The woman
comes to the window each day

to watch that lone rag wave
not truce, but luck, blood luck,

a single body not cast off,
no matter the odds.

TRUE GEOMETRY

Bless the sky for not falling
down, for being, in fact

a sprung umbrella, all spokes
blown upward inviting

grand swaths of light.
Bless the smack of wind

in your eyes while you hiked,
and the powerful push of it

against your van on its late
drive back. Bless the dark

through which your beams
cut, and your eyes for seeing

nearly unreadable signs.
Bless the crunch of gravel

that mumbled beneath you
as you pulled in, at last,

emptied of details, knowing
love was not a black and far

galaxy. Bless the one true
geometry of form and matter

which has nothing to do
with the way your shoes fell

near mine beside the bed,
nor the difficult angles

they assumed.

WHY I LOVE OYSTERS

Their tiny three-chambered
hearts, their colorless
translucent blood…

I love that they are true hermaphrodites,
tiny gonads surrounding digestive
organs like a ring of peeled grapelets,
apt to change sex one or more times
during an oceanic life.

Thus I am able to take both male
and female into my body whole
knowing as they slide into me
I eat the many possibilities

of sex, and it tastes like ocean
and body juices and I feel like a true
pure beast on the earth.

Bring them to me alive, sapid
in their nacre cups, aswim in their
liquor — with perhaps a dash of mignonette —
their throb bodies still humming.

When I tilt one in, life
and death will exist
in my mouth together,
as they will when
I inhale my last
unimaginable
breath.

ABOUT THE AUTHOR

Kathleen Lynch's first book, *Hinge*, won The Black Zinnias Poetry Book Award. Her chapbooks include *How to Build and Owl* and *Alterations of Rising*, both in the Select Poets Series from Small Poetry Press; *No Spring Chicken*, winner of the White Eagle Coffee Store Press Chapbook Prize; and *Kathleen Lynch Greatest Hits: 1985-2001* in the Pudding House Press Greatest Hits Series. Her poem, "Abracadabra", won a 2018 Pushcart Prize. Lynch won the 2019 Genosko Flash Fiction Award first prize. Kathleen lives in Sacramento, California.

ACKNOWLEDGEMENTS

Thank you to the editors of the journals listed below, in which these poems first appeared:

Ascent, "Nightwatch"
Carquinez Poetry Review, "You May Ask"
Chariton Review, "Prowler"
Comstock Review, "After Visiting the Cemetery"
Evansville Review, "Today Please, No Poetry"
Manzanita, "Late at Night My Sister Told Me Stories"
Passager, "Linoleum"
Perihelion, "Non-cinematic Departure"
Poetry, "Canned Food Drive"; "The Hard Season"
Poetry East, "History Lesson"; "Front Lawn"
Quarry West, "Sacrifices"
Quarterly West, "The Dream Speaks" (as "Dream/Not Me")
Runes, "Whistle"
Santa Monica Review, "Incubus"
Spectrum, "True Geometry"
Spillway, "Domestic Situation"; "Why I Love Oysters"
The Day's Motion, "Post-prandial Mood, Candles to the Nub"
The Recorder, "Jacket in the Back of the Closet"
Three Witch, "The Naturalists"
Tule Review, "Abracadabra"
Two Rivers Review, "Variegated" (first prize,
      Two Rivers Review Poetry Prize, 2002)

"Abracadabra" won a 2018 Pushcart Prize and appeared in *Pushcart Prize XLII*; "Farmer's Wife Turns Husband into Scarecrow" first appeared in the Chapbook, *No Spring Chicken*; "Impossible" first appeared in the chapbook *Alterations of Rising*, as part of the Select Poets Series from Small Poetry Press. Other poems in this collection have also appeared in chapbooks *How to Build and*

Owl and *Pudding House Greatest Hits: 1985-2001.*
Poems in this collection have also been published in the following
anthologies:

In a Fine Frenzy, "Ophelia in Utah"
Know Me Here, "Canned Food Drive";
  "Letter to an Unmet Grandmother"
Sacramento Voices, "Why I Love Oysters"
Times Ten, "Sacrifices"; "Incubus"

www.ingramcontent.com/pod-product-compliance
Lightning Source LLC
Chambersburg PA
CBHW032024090426
42741CB00006B/722